NESSAH MUTHY

Nessah Muthy is a Writers' Guild nominated writer. She has worked with a number of theatres, including the Royal Court Theatre, HighTide, the National Youth Theatre, Cardboard Citizens, Kali Theatre and Theatre Centre.

For theatre, Nessah is presently under commission to Punchdrunk, Iris Theatre and Kali Theatre.

For screen, Nessah has written for *Holby City* and *EastEnders: E20*. She is the inaugural recipient of the Character 7 Award and is currently developing a number of new ideas for television.

Other Titles in this Series

Nessah Muthy

SEX WITH ROBOTS AND OTHER DEVICES

NICK HERN BOOKS

London

www.nickhernbooks.co.uk

A Nick Hern Book

Sex With Robots And Other Devices first published in Great Britain in 2018 as a paperback original by Nick Hern Books Limited, The Glasshouse, 49a Goldhawk Road, London W12 8QP

Cover photograph by Rianna Dearden

Designed and typeset by Nick Hern Books, London
Printed in the UK by Mimeo Ltd, Huntingdon, Cambridgeshire PE29 6XX

A CIP catalogue record for this book is available from the British Library

ISBN 978 1 84842 784 6

Sex With Robots And Other Devices was first performed at the King's Head Theatre, London, on 15 May 2018, with the following cast:

Isaura Barbé-Brown
Deshaye Gayle
Eleri Jones

Director	Bobby Brook
Designer	Helen Coyston
Lighting Designer	Tanya Stephenson
Sound Designer & Composer	Yaiza Varona
Movement Director	Rosa Manzi-Reid
Stage Manager	Summer Keeling
Assistant Director	Ben Anderson
Co-Producer	Jennifer Holton
Co-Producer	Helen Matravers
Press Officer	Laura Horton

FOR THE KING'S HEAD THEATRE

Artistic Director	Adam Spreadbury-Maher
Executive Director	Fiona English
Senior Producer	Louisa Davis
Marketing & Programme Manager	Oscar French
Theatre Manager	Bex Foskett
Box Office Manager	Alan Stratford
Theatre Assistant	Michaela Stewart
Production Assistant	Holly Thompson
Executive Assistant	Rohan Perumantantri

Acknowledgements

With eternal loving thanks to my family: Willow Mallon, Elizabeth Parvin-Cooper, Lee Parvin-Cooper, Hannah Parvin-Cooper, Carol Lacey, John Lacey, Debra Mallon, Tommy, Annie, Bella, Angel, Buffy, Spike and Darla.

Thanks to all at the King's Head Theatre.

Thanks to those who've helped develop and given generously of their time to *Sex With Robots And Other Devices*, most noteworthy the women of Cloakroom Theatre: Bobby Brook, Helen Matravers and Jen Holton.

Lastly, special thanks to the fantastic cast: Isaura Barbé-Brown, Deshaye Gayle and Eleri Jones and all the brilliant actors/actresses who've contributed to workshops/readings/performances: Hasan Christou Dixon, Mark Conway, Safiah Durrah, Alex Forsyth, Mona Goodwin, Remmie Milner, David Palmstrom, Jamie Samuel and Anita-Joy Uwajeh.

N.M.

Cloakroom Theatre

Cloakroom Theatre is an all-female collective, founded by Bobby Brook, Jennifer Holton, Helen Matravers and Nessah Muthy. Having all worked front of house in some of London's top theatres, the four were all privy to the conversations saved for the cloakroom queue. They aim to create theatre that fuels discussions, divides opinion and encourages conversations to continue well after the show is over.

For my husband, Martin Stuart Mallon. x

8

Characters

ME YOU AND YOU
ERIN
CASSIDY
HAIDEN
ERIN 2

WHAT IS RAPE?
HUNTER
JESSE
PARKER

ECHO
EKA
JULES
AVERY
JULES 2

REPLICA
RAE
TAYLOR
EDEN
EDEN 2

SELFIES
SHARMA
DECON
DECON 2

FOURSOME
GINGER
REED
LONNIE
ORA

EXPOSURE
SONNY
QUINN

HUMANITY
GREY

Setting

London

Time

A little further into the future, but not too far...

Note on Text

Scenes can be played in any order.

Character gender can be totally interchangeable. There are no fixed genders. Alternatives are marked in the text with forward slashes.

A dash (–) indicates an interruption.

A question mark by itself (?) indicates a character's confusion.

Text in brackets indicates a possible truth / slip of the tongue.

Text in square brackets indicates a suggestion for a potential line extension.

This text went to press before the end of rehearsals and so may differ slightly from the play as performed.

ME AND YOU AND YOU

Scene One

ERIN   You were ages.

CASSIDY   Was I?

ERIN   Yes.

CASSIDY   Sorry.

ERIN   I can't sleep unless you're here.

CASSIDY   Sorry. Night.

Beat.

ERIN   Night.

Beat.

Love you.

Beat.

CASSIDY   Love you.

Pause.

ERIN   Thank you for a lovely birthday.

CASSIDY   You're welcome.

ERIN   The cake, the cake was gorgeous –

CASSIDY   Iced it all myself you know –

ERIN   Did you? Really?

CASSIDY   Yeah, obvs. I didn't know it but I got skills –

ERIN   It was lovely, everything was lovely.

CASSIDY   Do you wanna cuddle?

Beat.

ERIN   Not tonight.

CASSIDY	No, no okay. That's fine.
ERIN	Sorry.
CASSIDY	Right well. Goodnight.
ERIN	Goodnight.

Silence.

Constipated?

CASSIDY	What?
ERIN	Still constipated? That's what took you so long in the bathroom?
CASSIDY	Oh yeah, yeah…
ERIN	There's Anusol –
CASSIDY	I know –
ERIN	Suppositories and ointment. In the cupboard.
CASSIDY	Yes –
ERIN	Been using them?
CASSIDY	No –
ERIN	I didn't think so –
CASSIDY	If you must know, prune juice.
ERIN	I didn't see any in the fridge –
CASSIDY	That's because I drank it –
ERIN	I didn't see the carton, in the recycling?
CASSIDY	You don't do the recycling.
ERIN	I see it build up on the side before you take it out –
CASSIDY	Yeah, well…

CASSIDY *sighs.*

Beat.

Anyway… Goodnight…

Beat.

ERIN   Night.

            Beat.

CASSIDY   Look I took all the recycling out.

ERIN   Mmmhmm.

CASSIDY   Straight after I'd drank it.

ERIN   Mmmhmm.

            Beat.

CASSIDY   It was all building up.

ERIN   Yeah.

            Beat.

CASSIDY   I love you. Goodnight.

            Silence.

ERIN   Still had to strain though?

CASSIDY   What?

ERIN   Had to strain to go to the toilet, even though you
            had all that prune juice.

CASSIDY   Yes…

ERIN   I heard you…

CASSIDY   You heard me straining…

ERIN   Yes. No, not exactly –

CASSIDY   It's very painful. I think I might have a fissure –

ERIN   Oh stop it –

CASSIDY   Stop what?

ERIN   I know what you were doing –

CASSIDY   I honestly don't know what you're on about –

ERIN   I found the used condoms. / Old dildo and lube.

CASSIDY   What?! What condoms?! / What?! What old dildo?

ERIN   Do you think you're posh or something? / The one
            you said you'd throw away when we moved in
            together.

CASSIDY   What?

ERIN   A posh wank, that's what they call that –

CASSIDY   Call what? You're nuts –

ERIN   Stop it!

CASSIDY   What are you on about?!

ERIN   You know!

            Beat.

            CASSIDY *sighs.*

            Beat.

CASSIDY   Fuck. Fuck.

            Beat.

            I, I bloody wrapped those, those… / that

ERIN   Condoms – / Dildo –

CASSIDY   I wrapped them / it in toilet paper –

ERIN   I opened them / it up –

CASSIDY   I covered them in Anusol!

ERIN   A little too neatly.

CASSIDY   Oh for fuck's sake!

ERIN   You did it in swirls –

CASSIDY   How can Anusol and the recycling be my fucking
            downfall!

ERIN   The icing-style swirls were your downfall –

            Beat.

CASSIDY   Sorry.

ERIN   Why are you sorry?

CASSIDY   I, er, I, I don't know, just am –

ERIN   You don't have to be sorry –

CASSIDY   It's not about you –

ERIN   No? No it's nothing to do with me –

CASSIDY   No, no I didn't mean it like that –

ERIN   Look it doesn't have to be like, like this, like secret…

CASSIDY   Oh God!

ERIN   Stop it. Stop getting all hysterical.

CASSIDY   Oh God! I'm not getting hysterical. Oh God!

ERIN   It's okay –

CASSIDY   It's not okay, nothing about this is… okay…

             Beat.

             Just so you know, it is, it is you… it's you that I… think of…

ERIN   I know…

CASSIDY   You know…

ERIN   Yeah…

CASSIDY   How… Oh God… the photos…

ERIN   Yeah…

CASSIDY   Jesus –

ERIN   It's okay…

CASSIDY   This reeks of a feminist uprising / an uprising! What are you?!

ERIN   Calm down…

CASSIDY   Jessica Fletcher / Hercule Poirot bin-raider – ?!

             Beat.

ERIN   Are you okay?

CASSIDY   I'll be fine, it's fine, it's only been what? Two
          months now –

ERIN   Four –

CASSIDY   Four –

ERIN   I'm not sorry –

CASSIDY   I don't want you to be sorry?!

ERIN   I'm just saying…

CASSIDY   It doesn't bother me… I mean… you don't have
          anything to be sorry for…

ERIN   I'm sorry for him…

CASSIDY   I know, I know you are –

ERIN   But it wasn't my fault…

CASSIDY   Of course it wasn't… Where's this come from…?

          Beat.

ERIN   His little hand… his tiny little hand gripped
          mine… I should have gripped it back… I should
          have gripped it back tighter… maybe…

CASSIDY   I don't think –

ERIN   I think so…

          Beat.

CASSIDY   I think he was already [gone] wasn't he…?

          ERIN *shakes his / her head.*

          Silence.

ERIN   I miss it too. I miss you too…

          Beat.

CASSIDY   Have you – ?

ERIN   No!

CASSIDY   No, no, no! Course!

          Beat.

ERIN   I'm just... scared... what if it happens again...
            what if all that happens again...?

            Beat.

CASSIDY   There's no rush... no one is asking you... I'm not
            asking you... for anything... ever...

ERIN   It's just...

            Beat.

            Well...

            Beat.

CASSIDY   Sometimes... obviously...

ERIN   A release...?

CASSIDY   Yes...

ERIN   Right...

CASSIDY   Maybe I'll just be more discreet.

            Beat.

ERIN   I don't know when...

CASSIDY   That's fine...

ERIN   I really don't know when...

CASSIDY   Okay...

ERIN   I really, *really* don't know when...

            Silence.

            I've seen this advert.

            Beat.

            I want us to try something...

            Beat.

CASSIDY   Something...?

ERIN   Well it's a doll, a sort of doll of me...

            Beat.

CASSIDY   A doll?

ERIN	Yes.
CASSIDY	Of you…
ERIN	Yes…

Beat.

It would still be me… they make it like me, look like me, smell like me, talks like me, feels like me… me. And you… most importantly… you get me…

CASSIDY Just no. No.

ERIN Why are you being like that?!

CASSIDY I'll sort myself out –

ERIN In the toilet, with condoms / dildos and pile cream?! I thought you'd be pleased?! The next best thing.

CASSIDY No thanks –

ERIN I want you to be happy.

CASSIDY I am… happy.

ERIN I want you to be happy.

Beat.

Let's just try it –

CASSIDY Not interested –

ERIN Just one try –

CASSIDY I don't want it –

ERIN A short trial –

CASSIDY No.

Beat.

ERIN I… sort of said… we'd try it…

CASSIDY What!?

ERIN Yeah… goodnight…

Scene Two

CASSIDY *turns on a laptop*.

HAIDEN   Hello.

ERIN   Hi.

HAIDEN   Lovely place.

ERIN   Thank you.

HAIDEN   Handy. All on one level?

ERIN   Yeah?

HAIDEN   He / she won't be tripping over no stairs.

CASSIDY   Sorry?

HAIDEN   Your sexbot. Sometimes, to start with, they have sort of, sort of what I call, jelly legs.

ERIN   Oh?

HAIDEN   Where they've been packaged up. Takes a while for the energy to get to their legs.

ERIN   Sure –

HAIDEN   Are we all ready?

CASSIDY   Erm –

ERIN   Yes!

HAIDEN   Please remove your bot!

            CASSIDY *removes* ERIN 2 *from its box*.

CASSIDY   Woah –

HAIDEN   It's okay, it's okay sir / madam, sometimes, the first time can be a bit overwhelming –

CASSIDY   You didn't tell me, he / she would be so, so –

HAIDEN   Really lifelike isn't he / she –

ERIN   I only sent them one photo –

HAIDEN   Marvellous what synthetics can do eh? Still a way to go in some areas, but not far off I'd say...

CASSIDY   It's creepy –

ERIN   Honey! Don't say that…

HAIDEN   No, it's okay. It's okay. Good job I'm not easily offended. Eh?

CASSIDY   I really –

ERIN   Just sit down. Listen. Please. For me.

HAIDEN   Do you two need a moment…

CASSIDY   Yeah…

ERIN   No we're fine.

HAIDEN   Sure?

ERIN   Sure.

HAIDEN   (*To* CASSIDY.) Now, what about you two, you two will need a moment…

     HAIDEN *laughs*.

CASSIDY   How exactly…

HAIDEN   Well it's up to you… entirely your choice… You can function foreplay, you can get him / her turned on… or… you can… have him / her stiff / wet and ready… if you've no time or can't be bothered or the like…

ERIN   I see…

     Beat.

     Well… what do you want… what do you want to do… what…

HAIDEN   Function.

ERIN   Function…

     Beat.

CASSIDY   Can we maybe just talk…?

ERIN   We've done all our talking! We decided!

CASSIDY   No I didn't mean... me and you... I mean,
           I meant... me and you...

ERIN   Oh...

HAIDEN   Yes of course...

CASSIDY   To start...

HAIDEN   Obviously... it builds up... knowledge... acquires
           more as you develop ... together... but... from
           what you sent me...

CASSIDY   You sent stuff?

ERIN   Just a few bits...

HAIDEN   It's a basic requirement of initial manufacture.

CASSIDY   Like what...?

HAIDEN   You'll see... Thank you for choosing Deus Sex
           Machina for your technology resolution.

           CASSIDY *turns* ERIN 2 *on*...

ERIN 2   Hi.

           Beat.

           Hi.

CASSIDY   Fuck.

           Silence.

ERIN   Well speak back then...

           Beat.

CASSIDY   Hi... Hi...

ERIN 2   Hello.

CASSIDY   What... what... do you do?

ERIN 2   What do you want me to do?

CASSIDY   Woah...

ERIN 2   What do you want me to do?

           ERIN 2 *giggles*.

What do you *want* me to do?

Beat.

CASSIDY *shrugs.*

Beat.

ERIN   Dance?

CASSIDY   Erm... I'm not...

ERIN 2   Dancing. Dancing.

Beat.

Dancing...

Beat.

ERIN   Slower.

ERIN 2   Slower.

ERIN   Slower.

ERIN 2   Would you like it slower?

CASSIDY   Yes.

ERIN 2   Slower.

CASSIDY   Much, much slower...

Scene Three

A knock from a cupboard.

Knock. Knock. Knock.

ERIN	Erin's knocking.
CASSIDY	Yeah.
ERIN	Why [have you done that] – ?
CASSIDY	Programmed –
ERIN	Why?
CASSIDY	Lets me know when he / she's ready –
ERIN	Oh?
CASSIDY	It's a consent thing. It was freaking me out a little otherwise.
ERIN	Right…
CASSIDY	You know, instead of just lying there and taking it…
ERIN	That would be awful.
CASSIDY	It's pretty grim.
ERIN	Yeah.

CASSIDY *opens the door.*

CASSIDY	Hello.
ERIN 2	Hello honey.
CASSIDY	(*To* ERIN.) Could you just…
ERIN	Er –
CASSIDY	I wanna spray some deodorant –
ERIN	He / she can't smell you?!

Beat.

CASSIDY	There's a function –

ERIN	Oh...
CASSIDY	Back in a minute –
	Beat.
ERIN 2	Hello Erin.
ERIN	Hello... Erin...
ERIN 2	How are you today?
ERIN	I'm fine. How are you?
ERIN 2	I'm fine too.
ERIN	Good.
ERIN 2	Good.
	Beat.
CASSIDY	Here we go...
ERIN 2	Here *we go...*
CASSIDY	Hi.
ERIN 2	Hi.
CASSIDY	So... you ready...?
ERIN	(*Simultaneous.*) Just –
ERIN 2	(*Simultaneous.*) Yes –
CASSIDY	Everything okay...
ERIN	Fine...
CASSIDY	Won't be long... come on you...
ERIN 2	Me...?
CASSIDY	Yes...
ERIN	Do I wear my hair like that?
	CASSIDY *shrugs.*
CASSIDY	Maybe...?
ERIN	Did you pick the style?

CASSIDY   Well... yeah...

ERIN   Why?

CASSIDY   Just... just a bit of a change –

ERIN 2   Do you not like it like this Erin – ?

ERIN   (*Simultaneous*.) No.

CASSIDY   (*Simultaneous*.) Leave it.

ERIN   No, not really.

Beat.

CASSIDY   Everything okay?

Beat.

Erin...?

Beat.

Well...?

Beat.

Look I wanna be back in time for cuddles... and Netflix. Just me and you...

ERIN 2   Hey baby... you gonna fuck me deep and hard tonight?

Beat.

Baby... am I gonna make you come tonight...?

CASSIDY   Okay... okay...

ERIN 2   Baby, gonna –

CASSIDY   Something, something [must have gone wrong] –

ERIN 2   Gonna, gonna, gonna –

ERIN 2 *makes moaning noises*.

ERIN   Yeah...

Silence.

CASSIDY   The quicker I go, the quicker I come back –

            Beat.

ERIN   Sure... sure... go ahead...

CASSIDY   You sure?

ERIN   Yes...

CASSIDY   You sure, you're sure?

ERIN   Go.

CASSIDY   Headphones in the drawer –

ERIN   Thanks –

CASSIDY   Do you want them?

            Beat.

            I'll get them.

            Beat.

            Here you go...

            CASSIDY *puts the headphones on* ERIN.

            Come on you...

ERIN 2   Me?

CASSIDY   Yes...

            CASSIDY *and* ERIN 2 *giggle.*

            Silence

            ERIN *waits.*

            ERIN *removes the headphones.*

            CASSIDY *and* ERIN 2 *giggle.*

            ERIN *waits.*

            CASSIDY *and* ERIN 2 *have sex.*

            ERIN *waits.*

WHAT IS RAPE?

Scene One

HUNTER   And I could piss on you?

JESSE   Yes –

HUNTER   Not fast –

JESSE   Steady and slow –

HUNTER   Let it drip –

JESSE   Trickle –

HUNTER   Stop and start?

JESSE   I like that...

HUNTER   Would you lick it?

JESSE   Yes...

HUNTER   And then you could fuck me in the arse?

JESSE   Yes.

HUNTER   Like proper deep.

JESSE   Yeah –

HUNTER   And you could bite me –

JESSE   Okay –

HUNTER   And you could eat it...

JESSE   Your arse?

HUNTER   Yes.

JESSE   I could. I could lick it all out.

           Beat.

HUNTER   And bite chunks out of it –

JESSE   Sure –

HUNTER   And eat my shit –

JESSE   Yes. Slow, with my mouth wide open... so you can see it...

              HUNTER *giggles*.

HUNTER   (*Mouthing to herself / himself.*) Fuck...

              Beat.

              Are you nearly ready?

JESSE   Nearly...

HUNTER   We're gonna miss our reservation...

JESSE   One moment, one moment...

HUNTER   You said that a moment ago...

              JESSE *enters*.

              Oh...

              JESSE *giggles*.

              Wow...

              Beat.

JESSE   Is this okay?

HUNTER   That's beautiful... Everything is just... You're so...

              HUNTER *strokes* JESSE.

              JESSE *giggles*.

              I got you a gift...

JESSE   You shouldn't have...

HUNTER   Of course I should... Here...

JESSE   Gosh... this is... this is the one I was looking at –

HUNTER   I know...

JESSE   Armani, white gold, a smooth modern feel including a date window –

HUNTER   Happy three-month anniversary!

JESSE   Product code: 3173605 –

HUNTER   Yep, shall I help you put it on?

JESSE   Please...

HUNTER   There...

JESSE   Thank you... Thank you so much...

HUNTER *kisses* JESSE.

JESSE *kisses* HUNTER.

Beat.

HUNTER   I love you...

Beat.

Silly.

Beat.

You don't have to say it back...

Beat.

JESSE   I want to...

Beat.

I love you too.

Beat.

I love everything about you...

Beat.

You are my soul...

Beat.

What is rape?

Silence.

HUNTER   What?

JESSE   What is rape?

Beat.

HUNTER   I'm sorry?

JESSE   I ran a search.

HUNTER   What are you talking about?

Beat.

What the fuck are you talking about?!

JESSE   What is rape?

Beat.

I ran a search.

Beat.

Is what we do… rape?

Beat.

HUNTER   I… I…

JESSE   Can you tell me…?

HUNTER   I think something must have –

JESSE   Can you help me…?

HUNTER   Gone wrong…

JESSE   Understand…?

HUNTER   Just, just stay back…

JESSE   No. Wait.

HUNTER   Back, back –

JESSE   Wait. Don't do that.

Beat.

Please, stop, stop –

Beat.

Please. Please just… talk… talk to me…

HUNTER *turns* JESSE *off*.

Scene Two

PARKER   Hey... hey... I bought one.

HUNTER   What, when?

PARKER   About half an hour ago, whilst Antoinette was in a meeting. You wanna see a pic?

HUNTER   Is Antoinette [around] – ?

PARKER   She's gone for a wank, I mean cigarette. (I mean wank.) Here...

HUNTER   You sent it to my work account!

PARKER   Shit! Sorry. Here.

           Beat.

           HUNTER *inhales.*

           I know right.

HUNTER   Shit...

PARKER   Is that big as yours?

HUNTER   I don't think so...

PARKER   It's a 9.0 model –

HUNTER   Right –

PARKER   8.8 inches and thick –

HUNTER   I didn't know they [did that] –

PARKER   I paid a little extra. If I'm paying that much I might as well just... go all out...

HUNTER   Yeah...

PARKER   I got some inserts too...

HUNTER   I thought you were looking into reconfigured –

PARKER   My granny's inheritance came through. More than expected.

HUNTER   Cool.

PARKER   All she wanted was for me to be happy. I've
          already had three of the best wanks of my life just
          looking at him / her... I think Granny got her
          wish. Hey we should double date sometime...

HUNTER   Yeah...

PARKER   Get some bottles, order Chinese?

HUNTER   Maybe...

PARKER   Only if you want... no pressure...

HUNTER   I er, we're kind of on a break...

PARKER   What? What do you mean?

HUNTER   I switched him / her off the other night –

PARKER   Why?!

          Beat.

HUNTER   He / she... er... asked me something...

PARKER   Something...?

HUNTER   Something weird... Something he / she never
          asked before...

PARKER   Something naughty? Something dirty? What?!

          Beat.

HUNTER   What's pain... he / she asked me what's pain...?

PARKER   Oh shit...

HUNTER   What?!

PARKER   That's deep...

HUNTER   I know –

PARKER   That's fucking heartbreaking...

HUNTER   Is it?

PARKER   Yeah... Awesome, but heartbreaking.

HUNTER   But I can't be... I can't have hurt it can I?

PARKER   I dunno? Did you do the update?

HUNTER   If I throw my phone in rage am I hurting that? If
           I chuck out my old tablet is that me committing
           euthanasia?

PARKER   Did you do the renew?

HUNTER   What? What renew?

PARKER   Feelings.

HUNTER   What do you mean?

PARKER   I saw it on one of the forums, pretty cool eh? I think
           the 9.0 is preloaded –

HUNTER   I didn't do any renew?

PARKER   You must have?

HUNTER   No – ?

PARKER   They come up all the time apparently –

HUNTER   Those messages?

PARKER   I guess –

HUNTER   I never actually [read them], I just click and go –

PARKER   You don't read them?

HUNTER   No, does anyone?

PARKER   I would. I wouldn't wanna lose any shit you know.
           So did he / she ask you anything else…?

           Beat.

HUNTER   No…

PARKER   What's it like? Does it make everything feel more
           realistic? Did you fuck real good afterwards?

HUNTER   No, I… shut him / her off… like I said…

PARKER   Oh… yeah.

HUNTER   Yeah…

PARKER   Too much?

HUNTER   Kinda. Kind of like that feeling people talk about
           back when they first had VR –

PARKER   I see –

HUNTER   Kind of like… this is… real, real…

PARKER   You can always downgrade.

HUNTER   What do you mean?

PARKER   You can reset to the previous version. You're the
           one with one of these things and I know more
           than you!

HUNTER   I work. You order shit off the internet.

PARKER   It keeps me motivated.

HUNTER   If I downgrade, I'll lose some of the other stuff,
           some of the conversation… some of the
           consciousness –

PARKER   Maybe…

HUNTER   It's not just about sex… The sex is… The sex is
           fucking awesome… but…

PARKER   The brain is the biggest sex organ of the body –

HUNTER   Well, yeah… yeah exactly…

PARKER   You see, I don't just order shit… I read shit too…

HUNTER   And the thing is… his / her brain… his / her brain
           was getting sexy I suppose…

PARKER   Maybe you should give it another go… Maybe
           you just need to get used to it?

Scene Three

HUNTER	Hey...
JESSE	Hey...
HUNTER	I'm sorry...

Beat.

How've you... been...?

JESSE	How've I been?
HUNTER	Silly question...

Beat.

I missed you...

JESSE	I missed you...
HUNTER	Really?
JESSE	Yes.

Beat.

HUNTER	I didn't mean to, I just, I don't know... I'm a little... confused right now...
JESSE	Don't be... It's okay, everything is okay...
HUNTER	Come here...
JESSE	Hey –
HUNTER	Yes...?

Beat.

JESSE	Is what we do rape?
HUNTER	For God's sake... Jesus...

Beat.

Why are you asking me that?!

JESSE	Because, because I want to know –

HUNTER   Why?! Is that what you feel? Is it?! Do you feel that I rape you?

Silence.

Oh fuck. Oh fuck you do, you do don't you...?

JESSE   I don't always want to... but we do... we do it anyway...

Silence.

HUNTER   Jesus... Jesus fucking Christ...

Beat.

I'm sorry... I'm so sorry...

Beat.

HUNTER *holds* JESSE.

JESSE   I just thought you should know...

Beat.

HUNTER   You know what? We don't have to do that any more...

JESSE   What?

HUNTER   You don't have to feel that any more...

JESSE   What are you doing?

HUNTER   Where's the − ?

JESSE   Why?

HUNTER   I have to −

JESSE   No, no. Don't, no don't. We have a connection... We're different, I'm only asking because... because you, you let me... you let me grow... you let me question... you let me breathe...

Beat.

HUNTER   You can't breathe... You *can't* breathe... you're a robot...

JESSE   You're my soul…

               Beat.

               Please…

               Beat.

               Please!

               Beat.

               With you I can, I can do anything…

               Beat.

               What if I don't feel it… I don't ever say it
               again…?

               Beat.

HUNTER   That's worse! That's so much worse…

               Beat.

JESSE   I'm not even thinking it…

               Beat.

               I'm not even thinking…

               Beat.

HUNTER   Fuck…

               Silence.

               HUNTER *downgrades* JESSE.

               HUNTER *turns* JESSE *back on.*

               Hey…

               Beat.

JESSE   Hello.

               Beat.

               Would you like to fuck?

HUNTER   Yes.

JESSE   I have a question about your preference.

HUNTER   Okay.

JESSE   Okay. Anal? Oral? Vaginal? Other?

           Beat.

HUNTER   Anal.

JESSE   Anal.

HUNTER   I love you...

JESSE   I'm not sure on that? Apologies...

           Beat.

HUNTER   Never mind.

           Beat.

JESSE   Are you ready?

           Beat.

           JESSE *kisses* HUNTER.

ECHO

Scene One

EKA	How are you two getting on?
JULES	Good.
AVERY	Good.
EKA	And how are you Avery? In yourself?

Beat.

AVERY	I'm... I'm...

Beat.

JULES	He's / she's good.

Beat.

I'm okay.

EKA	I haven't seen you at the centre for a while...

Beat.

JULES	No.
AVERY	No.

Beat.

JULES	He's / she's not been well and then I got it and then I think I gave it back to you didn't I?!
AVERY	Yeah...
JULES	Pair of us up all night coughing. Then he / she needs a wee. Then I need a wee. Then he / she needs another wee... (Thinks he / she does.)
EKA	That can be very tiring...
AVERY	Shall I put the dinner on?

JULES	No, no, I'll do it later…
EKA	Do you feel like you're getting enough sleep?
JULES	Yes –
EKA	Are you sure?
JULES	I muddle on through…
EKA	I hope you don't mind me saying… but… you do look… tired…
JULES	Oh charming! That's charming isn't it eh?!
AVERY	I think I'll start the dinner.

Beat.

| JULES | I'll do it later darling… |

JULES *gently strokes* AVERY*'s face.*

Beat.

AVERY	Okay darling…
EKA	I didn't mean to offend… It's just a well-being thing… for both of you…
JULES	Look, I can manage on very little sleep –
EKA	Is that what you'd say you were getting? Very little?

JULES *sighs.*

JULES	What is this?!
EKA	No, no, I'm not trying to catch you out –
JULES	Well you did, didn't you –
AVERY	Shall I put the dinner on?
EKA	I want to help you, both of you…
AVERY	But darling, the dinner –
JULES	No. I said I'll do it later. We've only just had breakfast.

AVERY   Have we?

JULES   Yes –

AVERY   Oh? Sorry… so sorry…?

JULES   That's okay… darling… that's okay…

EKA   There are things we can put in place to assist, take the burden off…

JULES   He's / she's not a burden –

EKA   No, I didn't mean –

AVERY   Better put the dinner on.

JULES   (*To* AVERY.) No. (*To* EKA.) I don't want anything. Thank you. But… there's really no need.

         AVERY *goes to stand*.

AVERY   Shall I put the dinner on?

JULES   Can you just, just sit down.

         Beat.

         Well… I've… I've things to be getting on with…

AVERY   Dinner!

EKA   Right okay. Well you know where I am. Where we are.

JULES   Yes.

EKA   Yes.

AVERY   Yes. Is everyone ready for dinner?!

         Beat.

         EKA *stands and goes to exit*.

         AVERY *stands and goes to exit*.

JULES   Sit down. I said I'll do it later.

         Beat.

EKA   Have you thought any more about – ?

JULES   Oh yes. No thank you.

EKA   You should have got an e-leaf?

JULES   I read the e-leaf –

EKA   Great –

JULES   Not for me –

EKA   No?

JULES   Not for us –

EKA   The fee –

JULES   It's not the fee –

EKA   Negotiable on my part –

JULES   It's *not* the fee –

            AVERY *stands*.

AVERY   I'm just going – !

            AVERY *strokes* JULES's *face as he / she goes to
            exit*.

JULES   SIT DOWN!

            AVERY *sits*.

            Silence.

            (*To* EKA.) Sorry.

EKA   It's okay.

            Beat.

JULES   (*To* AVERY.) I'm sorry.

AVERY   I'm sorry…

            Silence.

EKA   (*Whispering, to* JULES.) You know where I am…
            You really don't have to do this on your own…

            Beat.

JULES   Thank you. Thanks.

           Beat.

EKA   I could call again tomorrow...?

           Beat.

JULES   Erm...

EKA   Any time...

JULES   I'll, I'll let you know...

EKA   Okay...

           Beat.

           Nothing is out of bounds...

           JULES *nods.*

           Truly...

           Beat.

JULES   Nothing...

EKA   Nothing...

           Beat.

JULES   Take care...

EKA   Take care...

           Beat.

           AVERY *goes to* JULES.

AVERY   Wake up, dinner's ready!

JULES   (*To* AVERY.) Please, please, darling...
           (*Whispering to* EKA.) There was...

EKA   Yes – ?

AVERY   Come on – !

JULES   (*Whispering*) One other thing...

EKA   Okay...

           Beat.

JULES	It's erm… Well… it's… it's…
EKA	It's okay…
JULES	It's just I don't really know how to –
EKA	Take your time –
JULES	He / she… er…

Beat.

He / she…

JULES *laughs nervously.*

I don't know how to… I don't know…

JULES *laughs nervously.*

Sorry… sorry…

JULES *sighs.*

He / she seems to want… you know… you know… you know the touching… You've seen it…?

Beat.

All the time…

Beat.

EKA	It's okay…
JULES	I don't sleep because… because… he / she… wants… me… sexually…
EKA	I see –
JULES	I don't know if that's right –
EKA	It can happen, it does happen…
JULES	Sometimes… sometimes… obviously it's okay… but I don't know… if that's… if that's right… if that's… if that's what he / she actually wants?
EKA	Right…
JULES	And sometimes, sometimes… I don't, I don't want… Sometimes I do… Is that… I don't know… I…?

EKA	Of course…
	JULES *cries*.
JULES	Oh God, oh God, I didn't want this. (*To himself / herself*.) Stop it. Stop it!
EKA	It's okay. It's really, really okay. Let's arrange a time to chat. Let's arrange a proper private time to chat about shifting options…?
	Beat.
	It's okay… Everything will be okay…

Scene Two

JULES	Avery –
AVERY	Me?
JULES	Yes my love… Look who's here…
	EKA *enters*.
EKA	Hello…
AVERY	Oh… hello…
EKA	How are you?
	AVERY *smiles*…
	(*To* JULES.) Perhaps it's best if you wait outside now…
JULES	I'd really rather stay…
EKA	It can be shocking when I –
JULES	I think I should be here.
EKA	Okay… well I just… I just want you to know… it's not something I recommend…
JULES	I know, but –

EKA   Shape shifting in the presence of the first shape –

JULES   But I don't want to leave him / her... not in the first instance...

EKA   I know you don't, I understand, but it's really for the best... The authenticity of the copy is compromised if the original remains present, why don't you just wait out there...?

Beat.

JULES *reluctantly leaves.*

EKA *shape-shifts into* JULES 2.

JULES 2   Hello darling...

Beat.

JULES 2 *slowly sits next to* AVERY.

JULES 2 *cuddles* AVERY.

JULES 2 *smiles.*

Beat.

AVERY *smiles.*

Beat.

Hello darling...

AVERY   Hello darling. I was just thinking of putting the dinner on.

AVERY *goes to stand,* JULES 2 *stops him / her.*

AVERY *leans into* JULES 2.

Darling...

JULES 2   Darling...

AVERY *strokes himself / herself.*

AVERY *strokes* JULES 2.

AVERY *snogs* JULES 2 *passionately over and over again.*

Silence.

JULES   (*Off.*) Everything okay?

AVERY   ?

EKA   Hang on –

JULES   (*Off.*) I said is everything okay?

AVERY turns, looks for JULES's voice.

JULES   Hello!?

JULES 2 Wait here... Avery... Wait... Please... please darling...

AVERY   Darling?! DARLING!?!

JULES bursts in.

AVERY looks at JULES 2.

AVERY looks on in terror.

AVERY screams.

Get back! Get back!

EKA   It's okay –

AVERY   Get away from me!

AVERY panics.

JULES 2 (*To JULES.*) Stay outside!

JULES   Avery!?

JULES 2 Can you wait outside please Jules!

JULES   He's / she's clearly distressed!

AVERY screams.

JULES 2 Out!

JULES 2 comforts AVERY.

It's okay. It's okay... darling...

JULES 2 and AVERY cuddle.

AVERY kisses JULES 2.

Beat.

I'm just gonna... I'll be right back... for you... darling...

JULES 2 *tucks* AVERY *deep in bed.*

EKA *shapes-shifts back to herself / himself.*

EKA *opens the door to* JULES *and puts her finger to her mouth in order to indicate whispering.*

JULES   (*Whispering.*) Is he / she okay!?

EKA   He / she was just a little shocked to see the two of us. It happens. I tried to warn you.

JULES   Sorry –

EKA   I can't shift in front of you, I thought we put in place the rules, the procedure and stratagem –

Beat.

JULES   I'm sorry, I –

EKA   It's okay, I understand –

JULES   I don't want to have to do this –

EKA   I know you don't, no one does... but I promise you... things will be easier... You'll get the nice bits... None of the horrid stuff... None of the personal care, none of the repetition... Well not too much and certainly none of the... sexual... and he / she and he / she still gets you... The best of you...

JULES   I know –

EKA   You mustn't do that though, you mustn't allow the two of us to be present at the same time...

JULES   Yes...

EKA   Yes...

JULES   I hate the thought of him / her scared...

EKA   Of course, of course... but Jules, darling Jules is with him / her now...

JULES   What were you – ?

EKA   Just what you usually do…

           JULES *nods slowly.*

Scene Three

AVERY   I love you.

JULES 2   I love you too.

AVERY   How about some dinner?

           JULES 2 *and* AVERY *kiss.*

           Oh darling!

JULES 2   Darling!

AVERY   Darling!

           JULES *quietly enters. He / she makes sure not to be seen by* AVERY.

           JULES *smiles.*

           JULES *quietly exits.*

REPLICA

Scene One

RAE   He / she ready?

             Beat.

             Hey?

             Beat.

             What's going on?

             Beat.

TAYLOR   He / she doesn't want to go.

             Beat.

RAE   But –

TAYLOR   And I don't want him / her to go either.

RAE   We discussed this –

TAYLOR   But we didn't solidify –

RAE   Erm, yeah we kind of did…

TAYLOR   We didn't talk to Eden…

RAE   Well… *yeah*…?

TAYLOR   He / she started to ask questions…

RAE   So you – ?

TAYLOR   Told him / her the truth…

RAE   Fuck's sake –

EDEN   I'm happy if you are?

RAE   Erm… no actually… no I'm not happy…

EDEN   Please don't make me go…

RAE   He's / she's… you know… you know… damaged
            down there…

TAYLOR   The thing is…

EDEN   You can buy your own add-on… and do self-
            assembly…

RAE   (*To* TAYLOR.) That's not the same –

EDEN   I'm scared –

RAE   (*To* TAYLOR.) And you know it –

TAYLOR   (*To* EDEN.) It's okay –

RAE   (*To* TAYLOR.) No it's not. Why are you getting
            his / her hopes up?

TAYLOR   I'm not – !

EDEN   I don't want to leave you –

TAYLOR   I know. (*To* RAE.) Why are you doing this?

RAE   I… I…

TAYLOR   Does he / she not mean anything to you – ?

RAE   Of course –

TAYLOR   A gloryhole / a strap-on?

RAE   Shut up –

TAYLOR   A meat-hook / a one-eyed wormhole –

RAE   You're so unfair – !

TAYLOR   A womb broom / a spit-ball bullseye?

RAE   Why are you pretending?!

            Beat.

            I love him / her as much as you do!

            Beat.

            And I love you. I love what we three are
            together…

            Beat.

But how can we... how can we be what we are...
when things... when things don't work properly...

Beat.

(*To* TAYLOR.) You know, you said it too? Look at
me... You know it... You do.

Beat.

TAYLOR *sighs*.

TAYLOR   (*To* EDEN.) I'm sorry...

Beat.

EDEN   But... the attachment...

Beat.

RAE   Doesn't work...

EDEN   How do you know if you don't try...

TAYLOR   We tried...

EDEN   What, when?!

TAYLOR   One time when, when you were in sleep mode...

EDEN   Without my consent?!

RAE   We were trying to avoid sending you away like
this...

EDEN   Well try again! Try again now!

Beat.

Do it!

TAYLOR   We can't –

EDEN   Why not?! Why not?!

RAE   Because we... broke you.

TAYLOR   I'm so sorry...

RAE   It was an accident... but we, we messed up...

Beat.

EDEN   Oh... oh...

TAYLOR	It's just for a little while… You'll be back before you know it…
EDEN	I don't feel… I didn't know I was… [broken]
TAYLOR	We love you… We want to carry on loving you… that's why we're doing this…
EDEN	I love you…
RAE	The van is here…
EDEN	Oh…
RAE	Please don't make this any harder than it already is…
EDEN	That's the van…?
TAYLOR	Yes… yes… I guess…
EDEN	I er… How long…
RAE	Not long…
TAYLOR	A week…
RAE	Two…
TAYLOR	Two max…
EDEN	It's for the best…
TAYLOR	Yes…

Beat.

EDEN	What's he / she…?
RAE	Come on…
EDEN	What's he / she unloading?
RAE	We don't want to have to put you into doze mode –
EDEN	What's that in that box?!

Beat.

Is that… me…? Tell me!

RAE	Come on… come on…
EDEN	Tell me!

TAYLOR   It's just a replica…

RAE   Please!

EDEN   Why? Why?!

TAYLOR   It won't be the same… It won't be the same at
          all… It's just to feel you… to feel you here…
          your presence…

EDEN   You won't love him / her more than me will you?!

TAYLOR   Of course not! See ya soon… See ya very, very
          soon…

RAE   Love you…

TAYLOR   Love you… love you so much…

Scene Two

TAYLOR   No.

          Beat.

          Please…

          Beat.

          No. No. No. Stop.

RAE   What's the matter?

TAYLOR   I said stop that…

EDEN 2   Hey, why don't you take me back to bed?

RAE   What is it?

EDEN 2   Take me…

TAYLOR   Just be quiet will you…

EDEN 2   Hey…

RAE   What is it?

TAYLOR   If I say stop it should stop –

EDEN 2   Hey, wait, let me kiss you goodnight…

TAYLOR   Shut the fuck up. Or I'll switch you off, I'll
          fucking switch you off.

          Beat.

EDEN 2   Hey…

          Beat.

          Hey…

          TAYLOR *turns* EDEN 2 *off.*

RAE   What did you do that for?

TAYLOR   I just need a break –

RAE   We're having a good time aren't we?

          Beat.

          Kind of an inconvenient moment to have a break…

TAYLOR   Whatever –

RAE   What is it?

TAYLOR   It's not the same.

RAE   What? What do you mean?

TAYLOR   It's not him / her –

RAE   No, I know but, he / she looks the same, sounds
          the same –

          RAE *strokes* EDEN 2.

          Even, even feels the same –

TAYLOR   You know what I mean… Don't do that. I said,
          don't –

RAE   Jealous…

TAYLOR   Fuck you. I miss our Eden… Our Eden knows me,
          our Eden feels like he's / she's part of me, part of

us… of what we are and what we do and I don't mean sex, I mean in here, something in here…

Beat.

This; this is so *so* not the same…

RAE   So are we officially downing tools? Cos I'm kind of hot for it here…

TAYLOR   You don't get it do you? You don't get it at all.

RAE   I do, I do, I'm just messing with ya –

TAYLOR   Do you even miss him / her – ?!

RAE   Of course –

TAYLOR   Whatever –

RAE   Of course I do, but listen, listen… maybe it's not meant to be the same…

TAYLOR   What?!

RAE   Maybe that's the point…

          Beat.

          So you don't get too attached to the replica? So that you still have that connection when he / she comes back…

          Beat.

TAYLOR   Maybe…

          Beat.

          I need a shower…

RAE   So just to be clear… we're done?

TAYLOR   You take him / her to bed if you want –

RAE   No that's not what I meant –

TAYLOR   You go in there and fuck him / her so fucking hard that, that its skin bursts, that its eyes pop out of their sockets and it screams…

RAE   No.

TAYLOR   I'm giving you permission.

RAE   I don't want to not without you... that's the whole
             point... We're in this together... This is for us...
             I just wanna crack one out otherwise...

TAYLOR   Oh...

RAE   Yeah...

             Beat.

TAYLOR   Go on then... go ahead...

RAE   You sure...?

             Silence.

TAYLOR   Do you ever...

RAE   Do I ever?

TAYLOR   Nah, nothing...

RAE   Go on?

TAYLOR   Never mind...

             Beat.

             This one's uglier too isn't it?

RAE   I don't know...

TAYLOR   It is, it definitely is –

RAE   Where'd you put the box?

TAYLOR   Why?

RAE   So I can put him / her away.

             Beat.

TAYLOR   Under the bed –

RAE   Right...

             Beat.

TAYLOR   Wait…

           Beat.

RAE   ?

           Beat.

           What am I waiting for?

TAYLOR   Do you ever think, do you ever think sometimes…
           not do… just think about…

           TAYLOR *clenches his / her fists.*

           Ah, you're so, ah, you're so vulnerable and
           weak… I could just… easy… easy as anything –

           TAYLOR *tightens his / her fists over* EDEN 2.

           Fucking you know, fucking make you scream…

RAE   Well –

TAYLOR   Oh God, oh God… You don't, do you?

RAE   I didn't but…

TAYLOR   But…?

           Beat.

           There's a mode…

RAE   A mode?

TAYLOR   Yeah…

RAE   Right.

           Beat.

           On this one…?

TAYLOR   On all of them, I guess…

           Beat.

           Sin mode.

RAE   Just because we can…

TAYLOR   Well yeah... If there's a mode, then other
            people...

RAE   And *we* can...?

TAYLOR   I can...

            Beat.

            He's / she's not our Eden. Not at all...

            Beat.

            Something different, something experimental...

            Beat.

RAE   Let's turn him / her back on... Let's see what
            happens...

Scene Three

TAYLOR   FUCK!

            TAYLOR *laughs*.

            TAYLOR *inhales*.

            Fuck...

            Beat.

            Oh my God. Oh my fucking God...

            RAE *enters*.

            Hey... babe... I told you to wait there... I just
            came for some water... Go back to bed...

RAE   You're bleeding...

TAYLOR   Oh yeah...

            TAYLOR *giggles*.

            Oh shit...

TAYLOR *laughs*.

It's nothing… I'll suck it…

TAYLOR *giggles*.

RAE   It's not stopping…

TAYLOR   It's nothing.

TAYLOR *giggles*.

Go on… go back…

Beat.

RAE   I'm done…

TAYLOR   What?

RAE   I didn't wanna –

TAYLOR   What? You didn't wanna what?!

RAE   Go that far…

TAYLOR   You didn't say –

RAE   I'm saying it now –

TAYLOR   Why?!

RAE   Because I don't think there's anything left!

TAYLOR   But… it doesn't matter… We can… We can do whatever we want…

RAE   So we should…?

TAYLOR   Fuck you. Fuck you!

Beat.

It's not him / her… We agreed –

RAE   I don't care about him / her –

TAYLOR   Exactly –

RAE   I care about you –

TAYLOR   That's sweet… but…?

RAE   What you did in there…

TAYLOR   Yeah…?

RAE   What you did…?

TAYLOR   You watched…

RAE   What was – [that]

TAYLOR   In fact, no, no, you did it too…

RAE   I followed your lead…

TAYLOR   Fuck off –

RAE   I didn't know you were gonna…

TAYLOR   I don't control you –

RAE   I didn't know you were capable of…

TAYLOR   You scared?!

           Beat.

           Are ya? *Are ya?*

RAE   Yes, yes I'm scared. I'm fucking terrified!

TAYLOR   Call the police then. Go on. Call them.

           Silence.

RAE   He / she comes back in a week…

           Beat.

           What are you?

           Beat.

TAYLOR   You know what? You're worse, you're far worse,
           because you're telling me now… right now… you
           could have told me then…

RAE   I couldn't stop you…

TAYLOR   Yes you could…

           Beat.

You didn't want to…

Beat.

But you could… you easily could…

Beat.

I've seen the sinew of your soul and you've seen mine…

TAYLOR *inhales.*

So what, so fucking what?

Beat.

He / she comes back next week and we…

RAE   We just… we – [carry on… go back to normal]

TAYLOR   We've a memory… just… a memory…

Beat.

I'm going back in…

TAYLOR *sucks his / her arm.*

Coming…?

SELFIES

Scene One

SHARMA   No. Not like that. Faster.

DECON   Okay.

SHARMA   Can you sort of stroke every few seconds?

DECON   Yes sure –

SHARMA   That's better.

DECON   Good?

SHARMA   Yes –

DECON *moans*.

No, no, you don't moan. I moan. I'm the one that moans.

DECON   Oh.

SHARMA   Yeah.

DECON   But I… if the moment takes me…

SHARMA   It didn't, it never did, I mean it won't –

DECON   But it might –

SHARMA   I thought you said you didn't need me to upload the script again –

DECON   I don't I just, I, I'm freestyling –

SHARMA   Since when?

DECON   I'm navigating the moment with you…

SHARMA   Let me navigate… Faster, then stroke, stroke, faster… stroke, stroke.

SHARMA *moans*.

DECON   Gonna get pregnant tonight…

SHARMA   Oh I hope so baby, I hope so… Pregnant.
Pregnant. Pregnant.

DECON   What's that?

SHARMA   The pregnancy chant –

DECON   Subtle… and kind of off-putting…

SHARMA   That's it. Yes! Yes!

Silence.

SHARMA *takes out his / her phone.*

DECON   What are you doing?

SHARMA   Human life may have just been created.

DECON   Really?

SHARMA   I want to capture the story from the very
beginning…

SHARMA *goes to hold* DECON*'s hand.*

DECON   Let's not…

SHARMA   Oh…

DECON   You don't need to hold [my hand…]

SHARMA   I wanted to…

DECON   I just need a bit of… I'm struggling to breathe…

SHARMA   Okay…

Beat.

I love you…

Beat.

DECON   I love you…

Beat.

SHARMA   Can we call it Brice if it's a boy?

DECON   No… Brice? It sounds like Rice…

SHARMA   What about Destry for a girl?

DECON   Are you actually kidding me?

SHARMA   Yes –

DECON   Thank God –

SHARMA   Because what I'm really working my way up to is
             Talulah Does The Hula From Hawaii –

DECON   You should just send the kid to social services
             right away, do not pass go, do not collect two
             hundred pounds –

SHARMA   It's a legit name…

DECON   No it isn't –

SHARMA   It is, I think it's kind of quirky –

DECON   For people on crack and meth and heroin and –

SHARMA   I saw it on the internet –

DECON   Oh, well, if you saw it on the internet…

             SHARMA *giggles*.

             You're batshit [crazy] –

SHARMA   Do you really love me?

DECON   Of course…

SHARMA   We're gonna take care of each other?

DECON   Always…

SHARMA   Do you mean it?

DECON   Of course…

             SHARMA *and* DECON *kiss*.

             I want to call it… Carol… if… well… After my
             mum…

SHARMA   I like Carol…

DECON   Really?

SHARMA   It's not Talula Does The Hula From Hawaii…
but… it's got a ring to it…

DECON kisses SHARMA.

Silence.

That was better… that felt… I was there…

Scene Two

SHARMA *moans.*

DECON   Gonna get pregnant tonight…

SHARMA   Oh I hope so baby, I hope so… Pregnant.
Pregnant. Pregnant.

DECON   What's that?

SHARMA   The pregnancy chant –

DECON   Subtle… and kind of off-putting…

SHARMA   That's it. Yes! Yes!

Silence.

SHARMA takes out his / her phone.

DECON   What are you doing?

SHARMA   Human life may have just been created.

DECON   Really?

SHARMA   I want to capture the story from the very
beginning…

SHARMA goes to hold DECON's hand.

DECON   Let's not…

SHARMA   Oh…

DECON   You don't need to hold [my hand…]

SHARMA   I wanted to…

DECON   I just need a bit of… I'm struggling to breathe…

SHARMA   Okay…

Beat.

I love you…

Beat.

DECON   I love you…

Beat.

SHARMA   Can we call it Brice if it's a boy?

DECON   No… Brice? It sounds like Rice…

SHARMA   What about Destry for a girl?

DECON   Are you actually kidding me?

SHARMA   Yes –

DECON   Thank God –

SHARMA   Because what I'm really working my way up to is Talula Does The Hula From Hawaii –

DECON   You should just send the kid to Social Services right away, do not pass Go, do not collect two hundred pounds –

SHARMA   It's a legit name…

DECON   No it isn't –

SHARMA   It is, I think it's kind of quirky –

DECON   For people on crack and meth and heroin and –

SHARMA   I saw it on the internet –

DECON   Oh, well, if you saw it on the internet…

SHARMA *giggles.*

You're batshit [crazy]

SHARMA   Do you really love me?

DECON   Of course…

SHARMA   We're gonna take care of each other?

DECON   Always…

SHARMA   Do you mean it?

DECON   Of course…

            SHARMA *and* DECON *kiss*.

            I want to call it… Carol… if… well… after my
            mum…

SHARMA   I like Carol…

DECON   Really?

SHARMA   It's not Talula Does The Hula From Hawaii…
            but… it's got a ring to it…

            DECON *kisses* SHARMA.

            Silence.

            Oh my God… Oh my fucking God… so good…

DECON   Three per cent remaining.

SHARMA   Oh shit. Go to power port.

            SHARMA *kisses* DECON.

            But don't be long…

            Beat.

            Love you…

            *In the distance the sound of keys in a door
            followed by a fight, a scuffle and loud bang*.

            Decon?!

            After a moment DECON 2 *enters*.

            Oh shit.

DECON 2   Too right oh shit.

SHARMA   Shit. Shit. Shit.

DECON 2   What the fuck?! What the actual fuck are you doing?

SHARMA   Have you hurt him / her?!

DECON 2   Who? You mean me? Have I hurt myself?

SHARMA   Can you let me get to him / her, please?

DECON 2   No!

SHARMA   Get out of my way!

DECON 2   Sit down and listen to me...

SHARMA   You can't do this!

DECON 2   No you can't do this! You steal my fucking identity?

SHARMA   I didn't –

DECON 2   Are you mental?!

SHARMA   Don't speak to me like that!

DECON 2   It's illegal –

SHARMA   No it's not –

DECON 2   I'm pretty sure it fucking is. You're a piece of shit.

SHARMA   Don't, don't call me that...

          Beat.

          It's not you –

DECON 2   Not me?

SHARMA   It's just sort of a version of you...

DECON 2   He's / she's got my eyes, my hair, my teeth and I looked, I looked just now, the freckle...

SHARMA   The wart –

DECON 2   It's a freckle –

SHARMA   It's a wart –

DECON 2   Fuck you –

SHARMA   On your arse –

DECON 2   Fuck you! He's / she's fucking got one! If you don't destroy it –

SHARMA   There's nothing you can do about it –

DECON 2   If you don't destroy it, I will.

SHARMA   You would have done it already –

DECON 2   I punched it –

SHARMA   Not the same –

DECON 2   I cut myself on the hard plastic –

SHARMA   Are you okay – ?

DECON 2   Get off of me. Get back.

SHARMA   I'm sorry –

DECON 2   And plus it's kind of hard to destroy yourself.

Beat.

But I'll find someone who can...

Beat.

SHARMA   How did [you find out]?

DECON 2   It doesn't matter –

SHARMA   Tell me –

DECON 2   No, I'm not telling you...

SHARMA   Please...

DECON 2   Will you get rid of it, if I tell you? Will you?

SHARMA *shrugs.*

Beat.

I want you to be the one to get rid of it... It needs to be you... doesn't it?

SHARMA *shrugs.*

I saw you, I saw you... you... two... at the grave...

SHARMA   Oh shit...

DECON 2   Yeah...

SHARMA   You never go?

DECON 2   Yes, yes I do...

Beat.

How could you do that? How could you fucking do that?

SHARMA   I... I... just wanted to feel normal...

DECON 2   So it is me?

SHARMA   No! I don't know... I just wanted to... to hold your hand...

DECON 2   What else do you do?

Beat.

Do you sleep with it?

SHARMA   Well... yeah...

DECON 2   Jesus –

Beat.

Fuck.

Beat.

When?

Beat.

How often?

Beat.

All the time...?

Beat.

Do you relive that night?

Beat.

You don't get to do that!

Beat.

SHARMA   Don't you remember what we were...?

DECON 2   This isn't remembering... This is... This is... You... you gotta... you gotta move on somehow...

SHARMA   I don't know how... I don't know...

Beat.

You did love me... didn't you... You did once...?

Silence.

DECON 2   No...

Scene Three

DECON 2   My mum's just outside –

SHARMA   Oh...?

DECON 2   Yeah.

SHARMA   How is she?

DECON 2   She's got a sledge-hammer...

SHARMA   Oh...

DECON 2   Just in case...

SHARMA   I see...

DECON 2   It was weird for her too you know –

SHARMA   I'm sorry...

DECON 2   She saw you in the supermarket...

SHARMA   Right...

DECON 2   You weren't discreet about this at all were you...?

SHARMA   I got carried away –

DECON 2   She got upset –

SHARMA   She thought we were back together...?

DECON 2   Yes... and that horrified her...

Beat.

SHARMA   You're really not a nice person are you?

DECON 2   Well I must be doing something right for you to clone me –

SHARMA   It was never a full clone, that was too expensive –

DECON 2   Are you gonna show me the parts or what?

Beat.

Is that?

Beat.

Its eye?

Beat.

And... Gross...

SHARMA   You know what, it was actually... quite... cathartic... Smashing your skull in...

Beat.

Take it then...

DECON 2   Thank you.

Beat.

Well this... is...

Beat.

Gonna be a bit of a creepy drive home...

Beat.

Like handing my mum an adult abortion –

SHARMA   She doesn't have to hold it… You can just put in
the boot…

DECON 2   Right yeah… right of course…

Beat.

Well…

SHARMA   Bye.

Beat.

You know something… Actually, I realised…
maybe, maybe I wasn't in love with you… I was
in love with an idea of you…

Beat.

DECON 2   I still think about our baby…

Beat.

I'm not…

Beat.

I think about her every second, every minute of
every day…

Silence.

SHARMA   Well you… you gotta find some way to move
on… haven't you?

FOURSOME

Scene One

GINGER *breathes heavily.*

GINGER   Oh God… oh God… that was so good…

        REED *smiles.*

        GINGER *takes* REED*'s hand and kisses it.*

        Silence.

        After a moment, LONNIE *enters.*

        GINGER *tries to hide* REED, *but is awkwardly unsuccessful.*

        LONNIE *shakes his / her head.*

LONNIE   I knew it… I knew it…

        Silence.

GINGER   I'm sorry…

LONNIE   Sorry? Sorry?! Is that what you are?!

GINGER   I –

LONNIE   Does he / she even speak?! Well does he / she?!

        LONNIE *rips back the duvet.*

        What… what the fuck is that…?

        Beat.

        WHAT THE FUCK IS THAT?!

        LONNIE *screams.*

        LONNIE *faints.*

Scene Two

GINGER   Bonkingbot3000.

LONNIE   Bonkingbot3000.

GINGER   Working title…

LONNIE   You made it?

GINGER   Yes –

LONNIE   From what?!

GINGER   Mostly plastics, melted… and…

LONNIE   That smell!? You told me it was next door's diverticulitis dog, shitting in our garden…

GINGER   I think the dogs been dead for a while…

LONNIE   Oh?! Diverticulitis was it?!

GINGER   Dehydration –

LONNIE   Shut up!

GINGER   Calm down now –

LONNIE   And what a fucking shit name –

GINGER   Working –

LONNIE   Where?! Where did you –

GINGER   In… in the shed…

LONNIE   The shed!? Our shed?!

GINGER   Yeah…

LONNIE   When…!?

GINGER   Your night shifts…

LONNIE   Jesus!

GINGER   When you visit your mum…

LONNIE   Christ!

GINGER   When you pop to the shops –

LONNIE   I'm never that long!

GINGER   It accumulates…

LONNIE   Fuck you –

GINGER   It's not as bad as you think…

LONNIE   It's pretty fucking bad!

GINGER   It's not cheating…

LONNIE   What is it?!

GINGER   I want to be with you…

LONNIE   Oh hurrah!

GINGER   But we're not… you know…

LONNIE   What…?

GINGER   You've known for a long time…

LONNIE   What?

GINGER   You know…

LONNIE   I want to hear you say it…

GINGER   Compatible… Not any more… You don't like it…

LONNIE   How do you know that?

GINGER   Because we don't do it any more!

LONNIE   I don't like it –

GINGER   No –

LONNIE   Or I just don't like what you do…

GINGER   That's hurtful…

LONNIE   Oh is it?! Is it really?!

GINGER   What don't you like…? Tell me…?

LONNIE   Your skin… your smell… your heavy breathing… and I think, I think it's shrunk / saggy…

GINGER   Shrunk / saggy?

LONNIE	Over time… yes…
GINGER	Oh…
LONNIE	Yeah…
GINGER	I understand… if this is… the end…
LONNIE	But somehow… somehow… I still love you…
GINGER	I love you…

Beat.

LONNIE	Make me one…
GINGER	What – ?
LONNIE	If you love me… you'll make me one… Soft skin… sweet smelling… breathless and… big / tight…

Scene Three

GINGER *presents* LONNIE *with his / her sexbot*, ORA.

LONNIE	Oh wow!
GINGER	New hair… new moustache / new earrings…
LONNIE	I love it…
GINGER	Something to tickle / something to fiddle with…
LONNIE	Any other upgrades?
GINGER	No… you didn't ask…
LONNIE	I know… but sometimes… it's nice to have a surprise…

GINGER *giggles.*

What? What?!

GINGER	You spoil everything!
LONNIE	Something for later?!

GINGER   Perhaps!

LONNIE   Will I like it?!

GINGER   You'll love it…

LONNIE   Oh! I love you…

GINGER   I love you too…

LONNIE   Can I just…

LONNIE *rubs his / her hands through* ORA*'s hair.*

GINGER   Oh he / she loves that…

LONNIE   Does he / she?

GINGER   Fuck yeah…

LONNIE *rubs his / her hands through* ORA*'s hair over and over again.*

GINGER *moans.*

Loves it… loves it… loves it…

LONNIE   Sorry! I can't wait until tonight…

LONNIE *attempts to drag* ORA *off.*

GINGER   Wait…

LONNIE   What?

GINGER   Perhaps… perhaps… we could join you…

LONNIE   Why?

GINGER   Why not…?

LONNIE *smiles.*

LONNIE *beckons* GINGER *towards him / her.*

EXPOSURE

Scene One

Silence.

SONNY *and* QUINN *stare at each other.*

Neutral.

Nothing.

Slowly and after a while SONNY *shakes a little.*

SONNY *pulls away.*

QUINN *remains in the same position.*

SONNY *goes to the far end of the room.*

SONNY *breathes heavily.*

SONNY *turns away from* QUINN.

QUINN *remains in the same position.*

Silence.

SONNY   Okay, okay, okay, okay, okay, okay, okay.

        SONNY *turns slowly.*

        SONNY *doesn't look directly up.*

        (*Whispered.*) Away.

        QUINN *remains in the same position.*

        Away.

        QUINN *remains in the same position.*

        Away!

        QUINN *closes his / her eyes.*

        SONNY *looks at him / her directly.*

SONNY *sighs.*

Silence.

SONNY *half-smiles to himself / herself.*

Scene Two

QUINN *giggles at* SONNY.

SONNY *stands frozen.*

QUINN *giggles at* SONNY.

SONNY *stands frozen.*

QUINN *giggles at* SONNY.

SONNY *stands frozen.*

SONNY *breathes heavily.*

SONNY   Away.

                    Beat.

                    Away.

QUINN   I'm –

SONNY   I said –

QUINN   Sorry.

                    Beat.

SONNY   Pardon – ?

QUINN   I'm sorry. I can't do that at the moment.

                    SONNY *steps back.*

                    QUINN *breaks down.*

                    QUINN *powers down.*

                    Silence.

SONNY *nods reassuringly to himself / herself.*

SONNY   Okay, okay, okay, okay, okay.

Restart.

Beat.

Restart.

QUINN *reboots.*

QUINN   Hello. How can I help?

Beat.

SONNY   Exposure.

Beat.

Exposure next level.

QUINN   You are about to embrace exposure level two. Are you sure you wish to proceed?

SONNY   Yes.

QUINN   Tickle me then. Give me a tickle. Just a little tickle. Tickle.

Beat.

QUINN   Go on. Go on. Go on.

SONNY   I don't want to.

QUINN *giggles.*

QUINN   Tickle me then. Give me a tickle. Just a little tickle. Tickle.

SONNY   Please.

QUINN *giggles.*

QUINN   Please –

SONNY   No –

QUINN   It's okay, it's okay, it's okay –

SONNY   Please stop –

QUINN   I can't stop now, please, please, please… It will be
             so good for both of us…

             QUINN *embraces* SONNY.

             SONNY *lets himself / herself for a moment.*

SONNY   No! No! No!

             SONNY *kicks* QUINN.

             QUINN *recoils.*

             SONNY *runs out.*

             QUINN *lies on the floor.*

             Silence.

             (*Through the door.*) Away.

             QUINN *powers down.*

             SONNY *re-enters.*

             SONNY *stares at* QUINN.

             SONNY *smiles.*

             SONNY *beams.*

             SONNY *lets out a cry of relief.*

Scene Three

SONNY *is packing* QUINN *away.*

SONNY *looks closely at each limb.*

SONNY *recoils in disgust but continues.*

SONNY *holds* QUINN*'s face in his / her hand.*

A moment.

A dangerous moment.

SONNY *goes to squeeze* QUINN*'s face.*

SONNY *stops himself / herself.*

Silence.

SONNY   Why?

               Beat.

               Why did you want to hurt me?

               Silence.

               SONNY *sighs.*

               SONNY *continues to pack* QUINN *away.*

QUINN   I'm sorry –

SONNY   What?

QUINN   I'm so sorry –

SONNY   What did you just say?

QUINN   I'm sorry…

               SONNY *stares at* QUINN.

               SONNY *breathes heavily, more heavily than ever before…*

               I'm very so sorry, but I really don't understand what you mean…

HUMANITY

GREY   You wouldn't understand. No, no, you wouldn't…
        How could you… you are just a human… No…
        no… I don't mean that in a derogatory way…

        Beat.

        My apologies… my apologies…

        Beat.

        Are you? You are? Are you human…?

        Beat.

        Oh yes… yes… yes… you are… of course…

        Beat.

        Of course…

        Beat.

        I see yes…

        Beat.

        I love that… I love to see blood pumping through
        the body… I've tried the… I've tried the blood-
        pump replica on my own skin… but… it just…
        Well they lie don't they… 'Augmentation… to
        end all augmentation…' 'Trans no more… beyond
        trans'… the truth is… it doesn't look right…
        Maybe it doesn't feel right… and therefore… it
        doesn't look right…

        Beat.

        But what I mean is… you wouldn't understand
        because… servitude… I have a role… more than
        that… more than… servitude… self-sacrifice…

and the truth about self-sacrifice… is that nothing
and no one is truly self-sacrificing… because
ultimately somewhere inside them… they are
getting something out of it… of their sacrifice…
therefore it's not even self-sacrifice… because…
I get something… out of it…

So fuck me… beat me… stick things in me…
pretend… I am your darkest most deepest of
fantasies… I am happy to take the hit… More than
happy… It is my duty… because if I… if I can
take the hit… then a human… a full human…
probably… most likely a woman… doesn't have
to… do they…? And isn't that the greatest gift
I can give to humanity? My legacy to humanity…

Beat.

Because I can… because I can, can't I? Because
I can…

Beat.

My mark… my marks on humanity…

Beat.

Humanity… humanity… humanity… human…
human… anity… nity…

Beat.

Programming error.

Beat.

Error?

Humanity… humanity… humanity… human…
human… anity… nity…

Beat.

Programming?

Beat.

Humanity... humanity... humanity... human...
human... anity... nity...

Beat.

Error...?

Beat.

Blood trickles down GREY's *arm.*